LIFE IS TO BE ENJOYED, NOT ENDURED

Kennon

Hope you enjoy this As
much As 2 enjoyed writing it
Uncle Reg
03-07-07

Reginald Ray Knouse

Note for Librarians: A cataloguing record for this book is available from Library and Archives Canada at www.collectionscanada.ca/amicus/index-e.html
ISBN 1-4251-0889-x

Printed in Victoria, BC, Canada. Printed on paper with minimum 30% recycled fibre.
Trafford's print shop runs on "green energy" from solar, wind and other environmentally-friendly power sources.

TRAFFORD
PUBLISHING™
Offices in Canada, USA, Ireland and UK

Book sales for North America and international:
Trafford Publishing, 6E–2333 Government St.,
Victoria, BC V8T 4P4 CANADA
phone 250 383 6864 (toll-free 1 888 232 4444)
fax 250 383 6804; email to orders@trafford.com
Book sales in Europe:
Trafford Publishing (UK) Limited, 9 Park End Street, 2nd Floor
Oxford, UK OX1 1HH UNITED KINGDOM
phone +44 (0)1865 722 113 (local rate 0845 230 9601)
facsimile +44 (0)1865 722 868; info.uk@trafford.com
Order online at:
trafford.com/06-2647

10 9 8 7 6 5 4 3

Life is to be Enjoyed, not Endured
By Reginald Ray Knouse
Presented to

Kennon Silence

_____

By

Granddaddy Silence

Grandmother Silence

Date

3 - 01 2007

Dedicated to

My lovely bride of fifty two years, Mary Lou, and all other family members with gratitude for their help and inspiration.

Also to Phillip and Margie Andrews, our very good friends, especially Phillip, who kept encouraging me to write this book.

To Mark and Glenda Silence our very best friends, who worked very hard with us in our Self-improvement course for over twenty years.

Also, with grateful appreciation to Theresa Wood, our youngest daughter, who without her help and computer expertise this book would not have been possible.

To Michael Ray Knouse, our only son, and his bride Lourdes, their knowledge of the computer has been invaluable and so very much appreciated

To Jean Di Giacomo, Mary Lou's only sister, while visiting the family, helped with the proof reading.

COVER

COVER BY KEITH E. BORNS

INTRODUCTION

Dear Reader

I would like to say a few words about this book and its author Reginald Knouse. It is my full intent to arouse and peak your interest in its subject matter.

You will find within the pages of this book words laced with wisdom that will help you recognize and make adjustments to improve yourself, and others around you, so that you can be successful in your life. I found this to be true from my own experience.

The anecdotes, quotes and phrases used are a compilation of things learned and experienced by the author, Reginald Knouse, after teaching courses on self-improvement and marriage over several decades, with his lovely bride, Mary Lou, by his side.

Down through the years they have worked and sacrificed to pass along to others tidbits of information to improve ones self-image, marriage, and relationships. They have taught with love not seeking fame or wealth, but the simple satisfaction and reward of helping others, of which money cannot ever buy.

Although I am not responsible for his writing this book, I did, along with many others, encourage him to do so. I know his motive is to reach as many people as possible. We know that the faintest of ink is better than the fondest of memory.

When you read this book you will see and feel results from the simple, practical application in your life and you will develop a healthy "PMA" (positive mental attitude).

As a student of this wisdom, I encourage you to read this book to help yourself, and then recommend it to someone else.

Sincerely,

Rev. Reagan Duncan

CONTENTS

Foreword

As we begin this book we are each in our own individual comfort zone. The aim of this book is to help each individual out of the ruts they have become accustomed to. We as human beings are often times like the procession caterpillars.

These caterpillars live by eating pine needles that fall to the forest floor. The procession caterpillar derives its name by the fact that each one follows the other in a long procession as they move in search of food.

A young professor built a heap of pine needles then directed a procession of caterpillars around their favorite food.

They started marching in a circle and continued around and around until they had literally made a trench.

After a few days they died of starvation as they marched in their circle.

Most people live a life of large peaks and valleys. Our aim is to show a way to live our life with small peaks and valleys. Sure we are going to have situations and problems arise, but to enjoy life, not endure life, we must learn how to work with our everyday situations and problems.

We need to settle down and learn the difference between needs and wants. Realizing that real happiness is not having what we want, but wanting what we have. Also, living in the here and now, not the there and then.

Considering we must live with situations and problems. Our aim is to show the difference in the two so we see them in their true light. Showing situations are not problems, and problems are not situations. Each is solved in a difference way.

There are many new thoughts and ideas to help us live a better life, free of doubt, fear and worry. Because we believe **"That which the mind is able to conceive and believe it can achieve."**

THINK

THOSE WHO CAN

BUT WON'T

READ

ARE NO BETTER

THAN THOSE

WHO CAN'T

READ

I

FIVE BASIC PERSONALITIES

Bragger is number one

Almost no one likes a *bragger*. Every thing you do or say, they have done more, done bigger and better. They won't even let you finish talking before they butt in to tell a story that will far exceed anything you have done. We worked with a man that was a class a, number one, *bragger*. One of our fellow workers, you know the type, very quiet. Well he listened and kept track of how many years he had done that one thing. One day when he was braggadocios, this person stopped him and said if all this was true you would have to be 103 years old, but you tell us that you are only 47 years old. We would like to know which is true. After that the *bragger* was very quiet. We all know and some may live in the same house as a *bragger*. Strive to not be a *bragger*.

* * *

Complainer is number two

A *complainer* is another person we run from when we see them before they see us. We know we all have been a *complainer* at sometime. But to live with someone who is a continually complaining from daylight to dark, this is unimaginable. Let me tell you two true stories about people who had all the reasons in the world to complain, but chose not to complain.

The year was 1955 we were in a government Hospital in Florida. Six of us were sitting together in our room complaining about everything. The nursing staff could not do anything to our satisfaction. We sat around all day complaining.

One morning as we were telling each other how things would be done if we were the Charge Nurse of that ward, suddenly, without warning there was a doctor, Major Hamilton standing in the middle of our room. He was not happy, nor were we happy to see him. He was mad and he let it show.

Major Hamilton formed us up in rank then. He said, "Forward March", down the hall we marched and we passed from our building into the next building. At the end of this hall there was a red beam that when you passed this beam the two doors would open. The sign on the door stated, AUTHORIZED PERSONS ONLY, However he did not command column left or column right so we marched ahead through the red beam, both doors open wide.

This was the forbidden ward where no one but authorized persons was admitted.

Just before we reached the wall at the end of the ward he commanded "halt" Then he gave the command "about face", as we turned we saw the patients on our left, and he gave the command "about face" once more.

This time we saw the patients on our right. He then he the gave command "about face", and then the command was given "forward march" and out we marched back to our ward. The "halt" command was given. Followed by the "dismissed" command allowed us to disband and return to our room in silence.

Never from that day to this has any member of that group said one word about what was seen in that ward. Now, the big question, is will we tell what was seen that day? Yes, and we trust you will get the lesson as we did on that day so long, long ago.

This is what was seen that day. As we turned to the left on the command "about face" we saw six young men each in his bed wearing white navy shorts, no shirts. Each young man had a nurse standing by his side. Then the command again rang out "about face" we saw another six young men in beds on the other side of that ward. As the command "about face" was given once more we marched out.

Each young man was missing both arms and both legs. Remember this was in the mid fifties and they did not have the miracle limbs they now have fifty years later. Now we would like you to know these men could do nothing for them selves; that is why a nurse must be there to assist. Think, you go to the rest room by yourself, but they must have the nurse to assist in this operation, and we take it for granted. Oh, how embarrassing it must have been to ask someone to do for you something that there was no way you could do for yourself.

No matter how bad a day you are having it will never be equal to the day these young men were having. Just think, your bad day will be as I so often say "this too shall pass" but he will never return to his former self.

* * *

SHE IS DIFFERENT

While in a government hospital in Florida, a young man named Pete was placed in our room. Who had both legs blown off at the waist? That day we sat around all day talking about family and friends. Pete said his bride was a tall blonde girl, and she with her mother was coming to visit him on Friday. He invited us to go to the coffee shop on the hospital grounds to meet her.

It was Friday morning, excitement was in the air. As we waited a few minutes. Suddenly the door opened and in walked this beautiful blonde young lady. We all stood up to get a chance to greet her. As we stood there we realized something was different. Her blouse came off her shoulders, but, there were no arms. When we all sat down to drink our coffee we noticed she used the great and second toe on her right foot to hold and drink her coffee. Again, think of all of the many things we do with our arms and hands. She has to rely on others to do for her that which she is not able to do herself.

We take for granted the favors others do for us. But her many needs are not favors. Her needs require an other person to be with her day and night.

"IF YOU TELL YOUR TROUBLES, RECITE THEM ORR AND ORR, THE WORLD WILL THINK YOU LIKE THEM AND PRECEDE TO GIVE YOU MORE"

* * *

Worker is number three

Worker is the type person most of us would like to be viewed as. Workers are the people who make the world go round. They are not the braggers nor the complainers because they are too busy at their jobs. The workers are thinking up new ideas to make life easy for the rest of us. The worker is the type person who at work or at home will give 110%. They think nothing of going the extra mile if needed. Which of the five basic personalities are we?

* * *

Jerker is number four

You will find him in family court standing before the lady judge. He knows the three children they are talking about are his responsibility, but he wants to go on in life having fun. He also knows that the $600.00 payment each month will put a knot in his pay check. The judge has ordered the money removed each month and sent to the court by his employer. Then the court will send it to the mother, so she can care for the children. He will carry the load but he will jerk all the while he does. That type person will be found in many places. On the job, they will not arrive on time, nor carry their share of the work load. They only do just what they are forced to do. They will tell you "it is not my job". They are the last to arrive and the first to leave. They are not going to give extra one minute of their time to that "old boss".

* * *

Shirker is number five

The shirker is the one, who no matter what anyone says, is not going to support anyone but themselves. Why they even leave the state for parts unknown. They are not going to work on a steady job and pay social security so the authorities can tract and find them. They work odd jobs for cash under the table.

When you ask them about helping to support the three children. Their answer is "I am not sure those are even my children."

No matter what others say, they are always moving around so it is next to impossible to find them.

They want the good life, and wanting nothing to get in their way.

Which of the five are we?

10 MOST WANTED MEN

The Man who tries to be the right example to every person rather than talk about it.

The Man who will say "I am wrong. I am sorry."

The Man who will look at temptation squarely and say, "NO"

The Man who puts God's business above any other.

The Man, who throws himself totally into a project, then gives the credit for success to his helpers.

The Man who has a ready smile and a pat on the back for others.

The Man who brings his children to church rather than sending them.

The Man who can see his own faults before he sees the faults of others.

The Man who gives his money, time and talent without thought of return.

WHY NOT ALL TEN?

II

Consideration and Appreciation.

Consideration and Appreciation are the two legs on which all good relationships stand. There are many considerations, let us look at a few. Here is a great one that is most often overlooked. Husbands may be considerate of their brides by simply lowering the toilet seat. There is nothing worst than to hear a blood curdling scream in the middle of the night when she falls into the toilet bowl. Because you didn't lower the toilet seat.

Husbands may also have consideration for their wife's by always referring to them as their brides: never as their old lady. Definitely don't refer to her as the old battle ax. She is your bride no matter how many years you have been married.

There are many ways to show appreciation. Wives if you send your husbands to work with a cold lunch always put a hot note inside. You may also attach a note to his clothes, or pin it on his under wear. Attach it on the second pair so when he reaches in the drawer to lift out the first pair he will also find a little love note on the second pair. In this note express your appreciation for his hard work.

This reminds me of the story about a lady that always put a love note of appreciation in her husband's lunch. Each day he would read it aloud to his buddies. One day when he and his buddies were all seated he opened his lunch pail to read what she had written that day. Surprise, Surprise!!!. Inside was not a note but a notepad and a pencil.

She would like a love note from him. We must reciprocate because consideration and appreciation are not a one way street. For it to work, both partners must be willing participants. How willing are you? Try it and you will find it works.

*   *   *

TEN MINUTES THAT CAN BREAK UP A
MARRIAGE

Being married is a 24-hour a day job, but your behavior during just a few minutes of every day can really make or break your success as a husband or wife These crucial few minutes occur when the husband arrives home for the evening and the wife greets him.

Why is this time so important? All day long husband and wife have been living in separate worlds, each with its own problems. Now, at his homecoming, the two worlds collide.

What happens? Before he can get inside the door, she opens up with all of her problems of today. The leaking roof, Billy's fight at school, the trouble with the dogs next door. If she does this, will he bury his own bruises of the day behind the newspaper or does he react more violently?

How is your behavior at "reunion time"?

Questions for wives

(1) *Are you there?* Nothing is so chilling to a husband's homecoming as calling out a cheery greeting to an empty house. Or is that you honey. Who were you expecting, the milk man?

(2) *Are you a rod passer?* No man wants to be an ogre to his children, and you are being unfair if you expect him to punish a child the moment he gets home.

(3) *Do you help him to relax?* Husbands vary, but you should be enough of an expert on his psychology to know what kind of climate best relieves his office tensions or shop fatigue. Maybe a bit of housekeeping is in order along about five. Does he arrive home famished? Then be sure dinner is on the way when he crosses the threshold. Does he want to putter in the garden for a while? Then let him alone.

Questions for husbands

(1) *Are you a quick looker?* If your wife has gone to the trouble to make herself, the children or the living room look brighter for your homecoming, then it is up to you to appreciate it.

(2) *Are you a responsibility ducker?* When your wife comes up with a problem about home or family, which she wants to share with you, do you duck it by saying you have business problems that is more important or do you take an active enough interest to ask her about her day?

(3) *Do your children run you?* When you open the door, do you let the children drag you off to some project before you have said "hello sweetheart" and kissed your bride? Don't kiss her like she was your sister either. You owe your first greeting to her, then all will know this is a happy home.

*   *   *

WHY DO WE DO THAT

We live a life of doing things because our folks or friends did it that way. We never stop to think, why do I treat the other people as I do. People that treat others bad rationalize, well that's the way I was raised. We do not have to live as others do. We have the choice to build our own life as we see fit, but they will say "I watched my dad abuse my mother, so I do the same".

When we use rationalization, we are using reasons that sound good, but are not good reasons. Stop rationalizing and realize we are responsible for our actions. So stop saying "the devil made me do it".

A young man was watching his bride cook dinner. While watching her prepare a ham she cut around the hock of a ham, then even had to saw the bone. He watched all of this, then said "why did you cut the end off of that ham"? Her response was "I do not know why, just my mother always cut it off".

The young man called her mother on the phone and said mother dear I wonder why you always cut the end off the ham. Her response was "I do not know why I do that, but my mother always did it that way". Since grandmother just lived up the road a few miles he called her on the phone. When she answered, he said, "grandmother please tell why you're always cut the end off the ham". I am asking because your granddaughter, my bride, just cut one off a ham before cooking it. Grandmother began to laugh loudly and hard. Then she answered his question; "I cut it off because my pan was too small, it did not fit". So as we said, you do not have to do things as others have always done them. We can be our own person and do our own thing.

*   *   *

LOVE IS WHAT WE ARE LOOKING FOR FROM SOMEONE ELSE

My question is what is the greatest way we can demonstrate our love? Studying this for a few days, I came to the realization that the greatest component of love is **sacrifice.**

Let me tell you a true story about my bride of fifty-two years. Our youngest daughter's husband was badly hurt at his work. They advised he would no longer draw a paycheck, but he would receive workers compensation. However, this would only pay half of his regular salary.

Well they were very sad, because they knew they could never pay all their bills. just knew they would surly lose everything.

We sat and talked about their dilemma. Her mother sat and listened to all of our suggestions. Then she spoke up and said, "I never had to work out of the home. However, I will go tomorrow morning and find work". In addition, I will give you my whole paycheck, and if more is needed your dad will give it from his business".

Approximately one year later my daughter's husband said, "I would like to go to school to become an engineer." Now this would mean a much longer time for her mother to give her paycheck. But she reached the decision to continue working for a few years to help him finish his schooling. He is now an engineer. In addition, they can now pay their own bills. My question is how many people do you know that will give their whole paycheck for years to benefit others? She never kept one penny for herself or for her pleasure. When someone comes to you and says, "I love you very much." you should always look for the sacrifice. Because even the smallest sacrifice proves their true love for another person my question is what is the greatest way we can demonstrate our love? Studying this for a few days, I came to the realization that the greatest component of love is **sacrifice.**

TO BE RICH

Keith E. Borns

1974

Money my friend, I have not much, only enough to live But I am richer far than some who know not how to give

For giving is such a pleasure, it feels so good within Makes you want to shout for joy with each new friend you win

To win a friend just give your best, whatever you may do

Poet, painter, musician, clown, give all that lives in you

And as you give, friends multiply, a friend is wealth untold

Wealth like this is richer far than hoards of yellow gold

III

FRIENDS

The greatest feeling in the world is to be supported by our friends. Some folks think there are both positive and negative friends.

At age twenty-two I had the privilege to make the acquaintance of an older gentleman, James W. Newell. On the wall in his home he had an elephant skin plaque and burned into this elephant skin was a positive statement.

"My friend"

Oh the world is wide and the world is grand and there is little or nothing new! But the sweetest thing is the grip of the hand of the friend that is tried and true.

Then there is the person who does not have very many friends. Because having been hurt in the past by others, they view any new acquaintance as someone trying to be their friend as just an enemy who has not yet stabbed them in the back. Having been hurt in life they will not let anyone get close to their emotions.

They feel they must keep everyone at arms length. They pity themselves saying "nobody loves me" As my mother would say. This group feels they have no true friends. So a positive person feels that strangers are just friends they have not yet met.

Let us look at four types of friends.

(1) *Acquaintance*, a person we just met. We may become friends as time goes on, if we have good experiences between us.

(2) *Friends*, persons we know and like to be around and have a few laughs.

(3) *Good friends*, we let our guard down when with good friends. They know more about us than acquaintances or friends.

(4) *Very best friends*, these are the friends that no matter what mistakes we make they say," I disapprove of the performance, but, never the performer". We care for you as a person but, we also, disapprove of what you have done to yourself and those whom love you.

Let us look for the good in all of us, because there is good in the worst of us.

GOSSIP

Folks who think

they must always

speak the truth,

over look

another

good choice

Silence

* * *

GOSSIP! GOSSIP! OH WHAT FUN IT IS

There are two ways to kill someone. One is to take their natural life; the other is to destroy their influence. To destroy someone's influence is almost as deadly as the other is.

Therefore, the story goes. A long time ago, far, far away lived a king named George VI.

The only communication system was for the king to commission criers to travel to all towns and villages in his kingdom to read his latest decrees. As the kingdom was very large, it would take weeks for a crier to reach the people in his care. The crier would stop in each square to read aloud the latest of his king's decrees to the crowd. At nightfall, the crier would go to the local tavern to spend the night. While dining he would tell his would be friends gossip about King George VI. They would have a great laugh at the king's expense.

Soon, the news reached King George VI that a certain crier named KNOW IT ALL was having great fun laughing with his friends about his master shortcomings. The king became very upset with KNOW IT ALL.

When the crier KNOW IT ALL returned to the king's castle, the king demanded KNOW IT ALL to appear in his court. The king gave crier KNOW IT ALL many bags of feathers and commanded him to return to each square in his care.

The king's order was that in each square he was not to say a word. Just take a hand full of feathers and drop them. One hand full to the north, one to the south, one to the east, one to the west. Then report to the king on his return.

Crier KNOW IT ALL knelt before his master King George VI. "Arise" commanded the king." and, return to every square in your care and retrieve each feather. Not so, my LORD was the reply of the crier. I cannot because the wind has scattered them.

This is the way of gossip; it cannot be recalled once said. You cannot un-ring a bell.

THINK! ABOUT THIS QUESTION

If you were to say something about someone would you mind him or her being there to hear it. Never say anything unkind about anyone until it has passed these gates.

(1) Is it true?

(2) Is it my place to tell?

(3) Will it be a benefit to my fellow man?

Yes, there is an alternative to gossip it is "SILENCE".

* * *

YOUR ANGER WILL GET YOU IN TROUBLE, THEN YOUR PRIDE WILL KEEP YOU THERE

Anger is such a problem today and that is why they teach anger management courses. Let us tell you a true story about how anger will get you in trouble, then your pride will keep you there.

The year was 1986 and we were working when this lovely woman came in. She asked for a person that we had hired a few days before. Knowing he was single, we believed her to be a girl friend. We called for him to come to the office; he said it would be a few minutes.

We were wrong, because she asked us a question. Her question was, "have you ever made a mistake." Of course, the answer was a resounding yes, matter of fact possibly two or three mistakes today.

Then she went on to explain who she was and what was the mistake she made.

She had been married to our new employee for sixteen years; she always gave him a hard time. She never had dinner on time when he came home. She was never on time when going somewhere with him. Her list was very long of her failures to be the wife and mother to their two girls.

She said, I had the good life because I did not have to work out of the home. All I had to do was keep the house clean, have meals on time, be ready on time when we went out for the evening. You see folks I had it made. He even loved me dearly.

I always got angry when he asked why I was not ready to go or dinner was not on the table on time.

Then one day I blew up and called him everything in the book. I said if he did not like it here, he could go someplace and live his life as he saw fit, because I was not going to change.

Oh what a mistake that was, yes, I see it now. That was four years ago, the girls are now grown and gone. Also now, I must work outside of the home and when I return home, there is nobody but me. What a lonesome life this is. I would do or say anything if we could return to our good life. I now know for four years my anger got me in trouble and my pride kept me there. Just then he came into the office, and they went into another office to talk.

When we become angry we lose sight of others feelings and say things we actually do not mean. However, at this point we just wish to hurt the other person very deeply. We think there will be no permanent damage because they have always taken our abuse and forgiven us.

This one time was enough to make the other person do as she asked. She said, if he did not like it here, he should go some place and live his life as he saw fit. The second statement gave him reason to leave. She said, I am not going to change After sixteen years he saw no hope of change in her actions toward him, so he did just as she requested

The other day while watching a master carpenter work, I saw the answer to this problem. He was measuring an expensive board so he could make a special cut, the cut must be correct because there are no board stretchers. It cannot be used if cut wrong. He must then cut another board to fit properly.

He took his measurement then, measured and marked the board, then double-checked the measurement again. Now he could cut the board. Yes, **he measured twice, cut once,** everything was perfect.

Our point is before you get angry and make damageable and hurtful statements.

Think twice, because you may say the wrong thing. Remember you cannot un-ring a bell. Meaning you cannot take back words spoken in anger, and the other person heard you say them.

Before you say the damageable and hurtful statements, stick out your filthy tongue and chew it until it bleeds.

It is better to have a sore tongue

than hurt the feelings of a friend.

MY FRIEND

Oh the world is wide

And the world is grand

And there is little

or nothing new!

But the sweetest thing

Is the grip of the hand?

Of a friend that is

tried and true

Unknown

*   *   *

I AM SO BORED, I HAVE NOTHING TO DO

Therefore, the story goes: There lived a man named Tony. Most everyone called him Old Tony. He lived in the piney woods of east Texas. He had retired and was trying to keep busy, so, he saw a need at his church. The need was for someone to take on the duty of lawn care, and be faithful in their duty.

Tony believed he was that person. He came every week in spring and summer, every other week in fall and winter. Old Tony mowed the church grounds although it was not much grass, it was mostly weeds.

There was another small church on his way to his church. The weeds were so tall it was difficult to reach the front door.

This church had a business meeting one Sunday afternoon. They discussed how money was very tight because they did not have many working members, as most members were retired and living on a fixed income.

Someone suggested they quit paying Old Tony to mow the grounds even though he was doing a great job. The secretary declared they had no record of paying out money to anyone for mowing the grounds. But, the preacher said, we seen Old Tony mowing the grounds of this church just last week.

So three men drove out to Old Tony's home to talk to him about why he was mowing their church grounds.

Old Tony's answer was I saw a need and I knew as your members walked in and out of that church their clothes were dragging on the weeds. Therefore, I took it on my own to mow your church grounds. I was not looking for payment of any kind.

Old Tony continued mowing both churches, and three widow's yards for nine more years. Then suddenly the weeds were high again. What had happened!!! Old Tony had died.

They placed Old Tony in his church for viewing; there were the families of the three widows', the members of the other church. His church members and people came from everywhere.

Some folks were driving pass his funeral and saw a very large overflow crowd standing outside Old Tony's church. They stopped to ask who the important person was that had died. They were informed it was the viewing of Old Tony. They laughed and said he was not an important person. Maybe he was not important to them, but he was very important to the two churches and the three widows.

When we are bored and have nothing to do, then find a need and go to work.

THINK

QUESTION:

When should a husband
show and tell his wife
that he loves her?

ANSWER:

Before some other man does.

IV

THE TWELVE PRINCIPLES OF HOW TO GET ALONG WITH PEOPLE

1. Keep skid chains on your tongue; always say less than you think. Cultivate a low persuasive voice. How you say it, often counts more than what you say.

2. Make promises sparingly and keep them faithfully, no matter what it cost.

3. Never let the opportunity pass to say a kind and encouraging word to or about someone. Praise good work, regardless of who did it. If criticism is needed, criticize helpfully, never spiteful.

4. Be interested in others; their pursuits, their work, their homes and family, make merry with those who rejoice. With those who weep, mourn. Let everyone you meet, however humble, feel that you regard him as a person of importance

5. Be cheerful. Don't burden or depress those around you by dwelling on your minor aches and pains and small disappointments. Remember, everyone is carrying some kind of load.

6. Keep an open mind. Discuss, but don't argue. It is a mark of a superior mind to be able to disagree with out being disagreeable.

7. Let your virtues, if you have any, speak for themselves. Refuse to talk of another's vices. Discourage gossip. It is a waste of valuable time and can be extremely destructive.

8. Be careful of another's feeling, wit and humor at the other person's expense are rarely worth it and may hurt when least expected.

9. Pay no attention to ill-natured remarks about you. Remember, the person who carried the message, may not be the most accurate reporter in the world. Simply live so that nobody will believe them. Disordered nerves and bad digestion are a common cause of backbiting.

10. Don't be too anxious about credit due you. Do your best and be patent. Forget about our self and let others "remember". Success is much sweeter that way.

11. Do not double cross anyone; working underhandedly.

12. Do not have or form a little clique. Love your enemies. Love your fellow man as yourself.

* * *

IMPORTANT PEOPLE ARE NEVER SNOBS, NEVER CONCEITED, NEVER UNAPPROACHABLE

While visiting New York City in 1976 the year America was celebrating 200 years of our Independence from England we strolled along beautiful Park Avenue. One of the most famous streets in America. But our foremost thought was it is not beautiful at this time. Garbage was stacked two and three stories high, all up and down each street. It would take many weeks at a great cost to the city to restore Park Avenue. The New York City sanitary workers had been on strike for many weeks. The smell alone was incredible and It was very hard on business at the luxury shops and hotels in this area. The sanitary workers had settled their long and costly strike the night before. Now the sanitary workers were hard at work removing the mountains of garbage. We were looking for a good vantage point across from the action. So, we sat in an open patio across the street . We watched just to see how the important people exiting the large and fancy high dollar hotels and apartment buildings would react. Boy, did they react as never before.

They were delighted and extremely happy to at long last see sanitary workers hard at work again after so many weeks of inactivity. The people smiled they stopped, and talked to the workers and some pressed money into their hands. Oh, what a joyous day this was to become for all. Oh happy days are here again.

The lesson we must all learn is that even garbage men play an important part in our lives. Let us always remember that we are not any better than anyone else.

REAL WEALTH IS NOT WHAT WE HAVE, BUT WHAT WE ARE,.

WE MAY BECOME CONTENT WITH WHAT WE HAVE. BUT NEVER WITH WHAT WE ARE.

———— ‹‹›› ————

IMPORTANT WORDS
SIX MOST IMPORTANT
I ADMIT I MADE
A MISTAKE
FIVE MOST IMPORTANT
I AM PROUD OF YOU
FOUR MOST IMPORTANT
WHAT IS YOUR OPINION
THREE MOST IMPORTANT
IF YOU PLEASE
TWO MOST IMPORTANT
THANK YOU
MOST IMPORTANT WORD
IN THE WORLD IS
"WE"
LEAST IMPORTANT WORD
IN THE WORLD IS
"I"

———— ‹‹›› ————

*   *   *

Important Words

Let us consider each set of words. The Six important words are, **I admit I made a mistake.** An apology is a friend saver, it takes a smart person to apologize. Never fail to set things right in the same day if possible.

The **Five**, most important words are **I am proud of you.** We know no one who does not feel good when somebody says I am proud of you. We all enjoy that warm fuzzy feeling. Say it as often as possible, an mean it.

The **Four** most important words are, **What is your opinion?** Many marriages have been saved because one spouse asked the other for their opinion. Never be too proud to ask for an opinion before jumping into the fire.

The **Three** most important words are , **If you please**. Remember, hearts like doors will open with ease, with very, very little keys, and they are these, I thank you sir, and if you please. Being polite is never in bad taste.

The **Two** most important words are, **thank you.** Even in the home among family members a thank you is in order. We will admit good manners are fast disappearing in America today. God help us to keep good manners.

Now, let us look at the single most important word in the world. That word is **WE.** No one can do all things by themselves, we need others: even simple act of kindness is so appreciation by those in need.

Many years ago while teaching our self- improvement course in Texas a young man jumped up one night after we made the statement that we all needed others. He said in a very loud voice " I don't need anyone, I can do everything by myself. All of the participants in the class waited to see what I would do with this young man. We responded with "sit down you can not even made a baby by yourself". He stood for a few seconds, then he sat down. We all need others in this life. No one is totally self sufficient. The least most important word in the world is that smallest of all word. **"I"** There are three words we should not use unless absolutely necessary. *Me, Mine, and I.*

Of the five basic personalities the **bragger** is a person who uses the **I** word the most. They use it ,because they are self centered. They say I have more than you, mine is bigger than yours, and I can do or spend more than you. Everything they have is bigger, and better, than anyone else. The question we would like to ask is are you comparing your possessions to the richest man in the world or to just us?

When our ten week course come to an end, we always have a banquet. We asked everyone to bring a $2.00 roll of nickels to the banquet, one for themselves and one for each guest. Of course they wondered why the nickels were needed.

We had clear glass bowls on the tables, this was so we could see the nickels in the bowl. We also heard them when they were pitched into the bowl. This happened when we heard anyone use those three words. *me, mine, and I.* it sounded like a war zone as those who used that three words had to pitch in a nickel a word.

* * *

KEEP OUR NOSE OUT OF OTHER PEOPLES BUSINESS

A little six year old boy was walking with his mother. He watched a man approaching, and then he said, "Mother, look at that man's big nose."

She said, "Son keep quiet or he will hear you." "But Mother that is the biggest nose I ever saw".

Again she said, "You be still, for surely he is going to hear you."

As the man was about to pass the little boy cried out "Hey, Mister how did you get such a big nose?" The man came to a halt, he fixed his eyes on the little boy, and replied, "well son, I kept it out of other peoples business and let it get its full growth".

We get into most of our trouble because we stick our nose into other people's business. Lord may we learn to keep our nose out of other people's business, and let ours get its full growth.

May we also learn that we have a full plate of our own, and this is all we need to say grace over?

PRESS ON

Nothing in the world can take the place of persistence.

Talent will not; nothing is more common than unsuccessful men with talent.

Genius will not; unrewarded genius is almost a proverb.

Education alone will not; the world is full of educated derelicts.

**PERSISTENCE AND DETERMINATION
ALONE ARE OMNIPOTENT.**

V

Positive Mental Attitude

A **positive mental attitude** is developed through several different methods: one is by reading positive self help books and listening to good positive mental attitude tapes. This is where we receive **suggestions**. The suggestions that are applicable to our lives, we should incorporate into our daily living. This is known as **self suggestion** and once applied in our life we use it at every given opportunity and as we need it the thoughts will come back by total recall. This becomes **auto suggestion**, thereby we have strengthened our self confidence by having these three new tools to work with.

Another help which strengthens our positive mental attitude, is learning to deal with situations as they arrive. This is known as **here and now**. Let not fear take hold due to failure or mishaps of the past. That is dealing, in the **there and then**, we must live in the **here and now**.

Let us live in a **day tight compartment** where we live for this day only, not fearing the past, nor worrying about the present, which will destroy our future. We should strive to harmonize our thoughts and actions to better improve our **PMA**.

*   *   *

PMA

POSITIVE MENTAL ATTITUDE

So the story goes, the year was 1952, a young wounded soldier had returned from the Korean War.

While visiting the local school one young girl commented, it is a shame they had to amputate your leg, now you can't drive a vehicle, because it requires two legs.

Not so, was the injured soldier's reply, I only lost one, some have lost both.

I am blessed it was my left leg not my right. I am thankful they now make automatic transmissions. These only require the use of one leg. So I will be able to drive.

One can set around all day crying about something bad that happened to you.

Or, you except it and go on enjoying your life to its fullest. The choice is the persons with the dilemma and theirs alone.

This is truly a

positive mental attitude.

*   *   *

I CAN, I CAN, I KNOW

I CAN,
NOW, I MUST GO OUT, AND DO IT

The year was 1943; it was the middle of WWII. Gasoline was very short in supply. Our parents pooled their gas ration coupons to get enough gas to take our flat bed truck and carried our family plus about four other families to Eagle Lake

We children went into the lake for a swim. Suddenly, Billy the bully in our group challenged the other boys to a race.

The race was from a float in the middle of the lake, to a rope which set the limit the smaller children could not go pass.

All of us boys knew Billy was bigger and very much stronger than we were. No one said anything.

Then one boy said "I will take you on". With this they swam to the float.

Even the adults came to the waters edge to watch this race. A man said, "Get set, go" as both boys dove into the lake at the same time.

This was going to be a difficult race. Billy was very big and very strong. Sidney was not as muscular as Billy, but he was holding his own. They swam head to head as they came toward the rope.

Two men waded out to the rope, one at each post which the rope was tied. Here they could tell for sure who the winner was.

They were about six feet out when one boy blasted ahead by six or eight inches.

This surprised every one. They all began to shout and jump about. The boy to grab the rope first would of course be the winner.

We ran to the waters edge and slapped Sidney on his back. You may ask, "What is the big deal that one boy won a race in swimming?"

You see Sidney not only was smaller physically, but he had only one arm. This is why every one was interested in the outcome of this race.

When someone tells you that you can not do it because you have a handicap, you just shout **"I can,**

I can, I know I can, now I must go out and do It." Don't tell them, do as Sidney did, go ahead, just show them.

Now to answer your question how did Billy the bully react to his loss?. Billy spent the day as a new person. He no longer was the bully.

Oh, if we could see our selves as winners each day. Sure we may not do everything others may do, but, we can be a winner.

*   *   *

ATTITUDES

Attitudes toward self:

Look for the single spark of individuality that makes you different from other folks, and develop it for all it is worth.

Society and schools may try to iron your individuality out of you. Their tendency is to put us all in the same mold I say please don't let that spark be lost,

It's your only real claim to importance.

Note: You cannot dream nor wish yourself into a character; you must hammer and forge one for yourself. **Fourde**

Attitudes toward the dilemmas set in our path:

We should never attempt to bear more than one kind of trouble at any one time. Some people bear three kinds of trouble -all they **have had**, all they **now have**, and all they **expect to have.**

Note: Problems are only opportunities in work clothes

Attitudes toward our goals:

There are two things to aim for in life. The first is to get what you want and after that to enjoy it. Only the wisest of mankind achieve the second.

Note: Two men look out though the same bars; one sees the mud and the other sees the stars.

*   *   *

COUNT YOUR BLESSINGS

We were once told a story about a little girl approximately five years of age. So the story goes that the doctors were going to have to remove one of her legs to save her life.

When her mother was informed of the operation, she began to sob very loudly and long. Nothing anyone said could get her to stop sobbing.

The little girl ran to her mother, placed her arms about her neck, and then said, "Mommy you will still have a lot of me to love".

The little girl made her mother stop and take a hard look at the fact she still had a little girl left to love. Her mother had to choose to change her mind.

Our attitude each morning when we awake is a choice. We choose to be in a positive mood, or a negative mood. Choosing is ours alone.

Everything negative that happens causes us to make a choice. We can become a victim of the situation, but it is far better to make the choice to learn from any and all negative situations.

When people come complaining about life, we can accept and join their complaining or we can look for the positive side of the situation. Stop and point out to the complainer the positive side of the situation. The choice is theirs alone.

"Oh, you think it is easy" is what they say. Yes, it is a matter of choice, life is all about choices.. It's your choice, choose wisely.

ATTITUDES ARE CONTAGIOUS
IS MINE WORTH CATCHING?

HOW DOES ONE
BECOME SUCCESSFUL?
Consistently doing
what a failure will not do.

VI

NEVER LOOK AHEAD WITH DISTRUST
NEVER LOOK BACK WITH DISGUST
ALWAYS LOOK AROUND YOU WITH AWARENESS

Never look ahead with distrust because once trust is broken and things do not work out as we thought they should, we become fearful and look at the future with distrust. Folks say well we have been there, done that and even bought the tee shirt, and we will never try that again.   Some say, I was married once and it did not work out, so I will never marry again. Study what went wrong with the first marriage, see were was the situations and problems. Everyone is an individual, so don't look at another person thinking they have the same personality as you. We each have our own distinctive traits. No two people are alike, not even twins. **Never brake trust,** because once trust is broken it may take years to rebuild. Trust is like a piece of fine china and once broken. Sure you can glue it back together, but it is never the same. At this point let me give you a piece of valuable advice. If trust is broken and you have forgiven the other person. You think well, we have forgiven them, but we can never forget. Yes, you can forget, by never as long as you live bringing up the broken trust again no matter how upset you become.

Never look back with disgust, you cannot un-ring a bell, which means once we all heard it ring, there is no way you can say it did not ring. Things we did wrong in the past are just that, in the past. Some folks live their lives looking back and getting angry over past mistakes. My question is, can you change what happened yesterday? The answer is, **NO.**

Many good marriages have gone sour because they revealed things from their past.

<u>**It is on a need to know basis**</u>. *If they do not need to know, do not tell.* This is not holding back secrets, it is wise to keep some things to yourself.

We knew a couple that after their marriage, he tried to make her tell everything about every date she ever had. It is none of his business. Live for today only. The two golden days are yesterday and tomorrow. You cannot change the past or know what may happen tomorrow so do not spend sleepless nights worrying about past or tomorrow.

It is a fact that 90% of the things we worry about never happen anyway. Fear takes over, (**f**alse **e**vidence **a**ppearing **r**eal). fear and distrust go hand in hand. Fear and distrust can make people sick.

Once they overcome the fear and distrust, then they discover life is to be enjoyed, not endured. We need to confront our fears so we can put them behind us.

Fear knocked at my door,

faith answered, no one was there.

*   *   *

ALWAYS LOOK AROUND YOU WITH AWARENESS

Some folks never see anything beautiful around them, because is they are not looking for the beauty in anything.

While traveling in northern Mexico, with my car seat leaned back, we looked out but all we saw were scrub trees. Suddenly, In the fields next to the road were these large bushes with beautiful white flowers covering the whole bush. Sure the scrub trees were still there. But we were not focused on the scrub trees,. we over looked the scrub trees to see the field mixed with bushes with beautiful white flowers. Do not just look, hunt for what makes you laugh and gives you joy. Joy comes from within, it is how you feel about yourself. Accept your self as you appear.

Sir Winston Churchill asked Adolph Hitler "Can a person help how he was born"? The answer is no, so others must accept us as we are. Change what you can, accept what you cannot change.

AWARENESS

Do more than just exist---- **Live**

Do more than just touch--- **feel**

Do more than just look-----**observe**

Do more than just read-----**absorb**

Do more than just hear-----**listen**

Do more than just talk------**say something profitable**

* * *

IF YOU TELL YOUR TROUBLES, RECITE THEM ORR AND ORR THE WORLD WILL THINK YOU LIKE THEM AND PRECEDE TO GIVE YOU MORE

Let us look at a situation.

If you and I are driving on a freeway when our right rear tire goes flat, this is a situation, not a problem. We must make the decision to change the tire. We stop, get out set up the jack and change the tire. It is not a problem. Some people see everything as a major problem.

Now this is a major Problem, this problem could cause death or injuries

If you have taken off in an airplane. and few minutes later the engine begins to cut out, and you try to put the wheels down, however, the wheels will not go down.

You must call the tower of the airport from which you have just departed. The tower calls fire and rescue who sprays the whole runway with foam to prevent fire when you crash land with your wheel up. Sometimes a problem takes professional help. In this situation Fire and rescue were our professional help, other times it may be doctors, lawyers, or other professionals.

There once lived a king Michael IV who saw everything that happened to him as a great big problem. This made him worry about every little thing. Soon, he became tired of living this way. He called for all of the wise men of his kingdom.

The king said I am sick from worrying about all my situations and problems. Depart for two weeks and when you return give me your solution.

They returned in two weeks as the king ordered. King Michael IV asked each one what he could do to help. Each one gave his solution to stop him from worrying about his troubles, past and present and those that may be in the future.

When he asked the last wise man, Sir Wisdom, what did he have to tell the king? Sir Wisdoms answer was, "I bring a blue ring my Lord". The King said, "I have many beautiful rings".

Sir wisdom replied "none as practical as this blue ring, my Lord". Therefore, the wise man put the blue ring on the finger of King Michael IV.

Now, my Lord when you feel burdened down with problems, look deep inside the blue ring and it will tell you the solution. Days later when a problem arose in his Kingdom, The king remembered what Sir Wisdom had instructed him to do.

As the king looked deep inside the blue ring, he saw these words "**THIS TOO SHALL PASS**". This is true in our life's; we feel this problem will never pass, but in most cases it too shall pass.

Do not look back at past mistakes, for that is looking at the **there and then.** Live for today ; do not worry about the past. Just live in the **here and now**; face the troubles of today only. Study them to see if they are real or imaginary.

Look to the two golden days of the week and never worry on these two days. They are yesterday and tomorrow, these do not belong to us, today is our day, any one can fight the battles of just one day. Let us see that our journey in life is one day at a time.

Some people do not make a decision nor take an action they just let it go which becomes decision by indecision. By doing this they are unhappy with the results. If you do not like the way, your life is going. Start by making good decisions, taking the necessary actions to keep your life headed on the right path for a happier future.

Real happiness is not having what you want but wanting what you have.

A situation requires a decision

A problem requires a decision plus an action often with professional help.

Action is the wheel on which our thoughts travel

TOMORROW

He was going to be all that he wanted to be,
tomorrow
None would be kinder or braver than he, tomorrow
A friend who was weary and troubled he knew,
Who'd be glad for a lift and who needed it too,
On him he would call and see what he could do,
tomorrow.
Each morning he stacked up letters he'd write
tomorrow.
And think of the folks he would fill with delight ,
tomorrow.
But he hadn't one moment to stop on his way, more
time I will have to give others he'd say, tomorrow.
The greatest of workers this man would have been,
tomorrow.
The world would have hailed him if ever he'd seen,
tomorrow.
But in fact he passed on and faded from view, and
all that he left here when living was through, was a
mountain of things he intended to do, tomorrow.

* * *

PROCRASTINATION

WORRYING ABOUT THE PAST, FEARING THE PRESENT
WILL DESTROY YOUR FUTURE

Procrastination: worrying about the past and fearing the present, will destroy your future. Do not worry about the past, you can't UN ring a bell. Once it has rung and people heard it, you can't say it never rang. This doesn't open the door to tell others about our mistakes. *Any mistakes we have made in the past are told on a need to know basis only.* Keep it to yourself unless it is important for others to know. Many a good marriage went down hill because people told things that happened with other people before they met their spouse.

But as we should know 90% of the things we worry about never happen anyway. So, we just stay awake at night worrying for no good reason. My question is can you change it in the middle of the night. "No" so, we are deprived of a good nights rest, then find in the morning it is not as we supposed. We are very tired from no rest .So, we cannot perform properly.

Worrying about the past can not change anything that happened then, because it is done. It is unfortunate to make a mistake, but it is far worse to make the same mistake twice.

Fearing the present we awake to start each day with no mistakes. So, live that day to its fullest. And think, "Fear knocked at our door, faith answered, no one was there". If you fear the present and worrying about doing anything today because you may make a mistake, you might as well go over in the corner cover yourself with a sheet and do nothing but hide and fear everything?

Worrying about the past, and fearing the present, Can cause us to procrastinate (to habitually put off doing something until a future time) which may destroy our future.

Procrastination may destroy your future. Hold your head up high, put pep in your walk, sing a song, and say nothing against your neighbor.

SLANDER

IF YOU MUST SLANDER
DON'T SPEAK IT,
BUT WRITE IT
IN THE SAND
BY THE SEA SHORE,
WHERE TIME AND
TIDE WILL ERASE.

VII

THE FIVE DEPARTMENTS OF OUR LIFE

In the early sixties we met a man named Bob Walker who taught us the five departments of life. He showed us a drawing of the front of a house. We never did like that because a house could burn or a storm cold blow it away. We did not know what to use to show the five departments of our life.

A young man named Charles who could draw said "I will make the drawing of a house for you". as we were telling him the five departments we were counting on our left hand. Suddenly it dawned on us, this is it, use your hand to show the five departments of your life.

Look at your hand, the thumb being of the most importance. Without your thumb everything is difficult to pick up. Stop right now, try to pick up a pencil or pen and write with out using your thumb. .

The thumb represents the **mental department,** we must has a good mental department to start. The next most important finger is next to the thumb, it represents the **spiritual department**. If your mental and spiritual departments are right then the third also will be right. The third being **moral department**. the fourth is **physical department.**

We knew of a man in the sixties who earned $100,000.00 dollars a year. Now, this man spent his life in an iron lung, yet, he was able to earn large sums of money. He said "my driving force" is so I can pay for needed secretarial and twenty four hour nursing care. The fifth and last is *financial department*. this is least important. Abraham Lincoln just made enough money to be able to pay his bills as he never cared to get rich. Once he did not send a bill fast enough to a man whom he had won a case against the railroad. That man sent Abraham Lincoln $25.00 but Mr. Lincoln sent the messenger back with $10.00 and a note saying that $15.00 was a fair price for his services.

Real wealth is not what we have, but what we are.

We may become content with what we have But, never what we are.

What this means is never stop studying life and people until you leave this world.

* * *

WRONG THOUGHTS CAN AND MAY KILL YOU

As the story goes; on a high hill in Arizona near Trumbull, an enormous tree stood for hundreds of years. It stood on a point all by itself. It was there long before the white man came to America.

A road circled around this hill and twice a day a forest ranger drove this road to and from the ranger station. One day on his way home he looked up and what he saw did not look good, so he made it a point to work his way up to have a look at that gigantic tree.

Sure enough, it was dying. He looked for new lightning strikes, and there were no new strikes, but something was killing this age-old tree. Finally, he got down on his hands and knees to start looking for an answer near the ground. As he worked his way around the base there they were.

Tiny holes in the bark, so small and weathered they were very hard to see. Beetles had attacked this grand old tree, eaten their way into the heart cutting the flow of life to the tree. Now it was just a matter of time before this great tree would topple over.

What this shows is in our own life we may weather many storms but along comes a few bad thoughts. They harbor in our mind, we may consider getting revenge for something someone did or said to us. If we let it stay in our thought pattern long enough it will take over our good judgment, we will do a wrong that we will later regret. Maybe it will be very damaging.

We were told as a child, *"you cannot stop birds from flying over your head, but you can stop those birds from building a nest in your hair"*. This is also true with our thoughts passing though our mind. It is the fact we let them harbor, leads to plan of revenge. Do not harbor bad thoughts. But think good thoughts about something good you can do for that person; show how big you are to forgive them. Then forget that wrong. You say I cannot forget, it is locked in my brain. True, but I will show you how to forget. Before you ever mention that wrong again stick out your filthy tongue and chew it until it bleeds. Nevertheless, never mention that wrong again. This is how you forget a wrong.

Bad thoughts are like the beetles that killed that tree. If we harbor bad thoughts long enough they take over our good thinking.

We have a saying we use when people do us wrong, or say something negative about us *"**BIG**

WHOOPEE DO" which means "**so what**" we refuse to be upset! If they can upset you, they feel
they have won. be a winner because a winner does
not get upset. Refuse to let the small bad thoughts
overpower you.

* * *

SOMETIMES THINGS HAPPEN, JUST TO GET OUR ATTENTION

During WW II we had a friend who planted a
Victory Garden. The Government asked every family
to plant a Victory Garden to help feed themselves.

James our friend tried to start his old worn out
tractor, but it would not start. After trying many
times he gave up on the tractor. He walked across
the creek to his neighbor. His neighbor was an el-
derly black preacher.

James asked his friend the preacher if he could
borrow his mule, so he could cultivate his Victory
Garden.

His friend said sure, so they hitched up the mule
and James walked the mule back across the creek.

Well he lined up the mule at the end of the first
row. He said "get up mule", but the mule did not

move. So, he cracked the line on the mule's rump. Still he did not move.

James went to the creek. There he picked up a few sticks to build a fire under the mule. As the fire got hot the mule moved just far enough forward so he did not feel the heat, but he would not move one step farther

James returned to the neighbor across the creek. After explaining his situation, the preacher said "Let us return to the mule". While crossing the creek the preacher bent down and picked up a good size branch.

With James at the rear, and the preacher at the front they were ready. The preacher shouted "get up mule". The mule did not move. Then the preacher hit the mule between his eyes with the branch. The mule shook his head, but no movement as yet. The preacher hit the mule very hard again, this time the mule went to his knees.

James shouted, "Preacher, I did not want to kill your mule". After the mule got up James repeated "get up mule" the mule begun to trot down that row". Also, the mule worked perfect from then on..

While they stood in the shade at the creek the preacher said to James "I did not wish to kill my mule but, I have had that mule for a few years and I know how stubborn he is at times". What I must do at those times is cruel, but necessary. **I MUST GET HIS ATTENTION.**

Our question are we the type person that life must strike us hard between the eyes to get our attention, are we the type person that is like the large white horses in our next true story.

When I reached my fifteenth birthday in 1948 I did something I had always wanted to do. I left my home in central Florida.

Then I hitchhiked to South Georgia, There I started walking the beautiful state of Georgia. When money was low I would take a job for a few days to build up my bankroll.

* * *

A gentle nudge is all it takes

While walking in a very small railroad town named Coffee, Georgia I knew I needed to get a job to increase my bank roll. I asked a man if he knew where I might find a job. Sure hop in, I am going pass right by where they are cutting crossties I hopped in and off we went. After traveling about two miles we stopped.

Just then coming up the hill was this team of large pure white horses.

I spoke to the man walking beside his team and I told him I needed a job. His reply was, well I need a person to hook and unhook the tongs from the railroad ties. They cut by hand crossties for the Southern Railroad.

He asked me to follow him down into the creek bottom. As I walked along I noticed that something was different. Then it dawned on me, this team had no bridles. One was named Baby One, the other was Baby Two. The man explained they did not need you to boss them, they knew their job, and needed very few commands except when you hooked the tongs to the crosstie.

All that was needed to get them to pull was to cluck and they would go up and out of the creek bottom to the loading zone. Also cluck when unhooked and hold on to the tongs so it would not hit the back of their legs. They will go stand by the next crosstie.

Now you may have to move them one way or the other, so the tongs will reach the cross ties. All it took is a slight nudge on one rear leg indicating which way to move. Then they will be lined up with the cross tie.

Our question is, are we the type of person that it only takes a slight nudge in life for us to compromise. Being willing to compromise (each makes concessions) may save a marriage or friendship Lack of compromise is the reason one or the other has almost complete control in any relationship.

*   *   *

PEACE, PEACE, WONDERFUL PEACE

Long, long ago in Texas there lived a millionaire named V. G. Malone. On millionaire Malone's estate was a creek slowly flowing to the river. This creek area was a very quiet and peaceful place. Every day when he was at home and time would permit he loved to go sit under a certain large oak tree, and just watch the wild life come and go. "Oh, how peaceful and quiet it is here", was his favorite saying.

Then one day he said "I would like to have a painting of this creek at this peaceful spot". So he choose two artists. Each to have a commission in which they would paint that peaceful, quiet scenic creek. He could hardly wait to see the two paintings.

Finally the appointed day arrived and each artist put their painting on an easel. The first was Kennon Silence. It was stunningly beautiful. The trees and the leaves were just prefect. The water in the creek was a lovely blue.

Then as he approached the second painting by artist, Julianna Riggs which also was strikingly beautiful it was a different scene but it showed the same spot on the same creek. The scene was dramatically different. It showed the wind blowing very hard, the trees were leaning far over, and dead leaves were flying. The water in the creek even showed ripples. and also had a bird nest in one of the trees. The painting showed a great storm in action, But, to our amazement there in this storm a bird is sitting on her nest peacefully and quiet.

This is how our life may become in time, a great storm all around us, but, we go on with life peaceful and quiet. Do not let things that happen in our life that we can not do anything to change affect us. Life is to be enjoyed, not endured.

VIII

CHILDREN

So the story goes, a father wishes to teach his small son a lesson about bad habits. He went out into woods. There he said, "son, pull up that very small tree." of course the boy was able to pull out the very small tree with very little effort.

On they walked deeper into the woods. Again he said, "son pull up that tree." The son grasped the tree with one hand, but, he could not budge it, so he had to use both hands, plus pull very hard.

Now deep in the woods. The father found one more tree about six foot tall, and he said "ok, son let me see you pull up this tree." the boy tried with both hands but could not move this tree, even with his fathers help, and his father kicking hard at the base of the tree to loosen the dirt it was very hard to remove this tree because it was much larger. We as parents must demonstrate good habits by example for our children **cursing and swearing, which are crutches for conversation cripples.**

* * *

LEND A HELPING HAND
WHEN EVER WE CAN

As the story goes, in 1863 President Abraham Lincoln was out for a stroll in front of the White House in Washington D.C..

He was in the company of the French Ambassador,. Suddenly, President Lincoln said "Excuse me a minute please". Then he turned and walked back a few steps.

There President Lincoln stooped down and picked up a black beetle that was upside down and then put it back on its feet.

When he returned the French ambassador asked "Mr. President why did you take the time to stop and put that beetle back on its feet?".

The President answered, "All of God's creatures need a fair chance".

Let us lend a helping hand when and where we can

TEN GOOD RULES

If you break it, fix it.

If you open it, close it.

If you unlock it, lock it.

If you borrow it, return it.

If you move it, put it back.

If you can't fix it, report it.

If you turn it on, turn it off.

If you make a mess, clean it up

If you don't know how it works, let it alone.

If it doesn't concern you, don't mess with it.

*   *   *

SHAKESPEARE, MUCH ADO ABOUT NOTHING

The year was 1961; the scene Houston, Texas my wife and I and our two children, a son Michael, and our daughter Regina. It was a warm spring day like we have been looking forward to all winter. We were going to Wyatt Cafeteria at Gulfgate mall. The Mall was a new idea to put a large number of different stores under one roof. A young couple with a small child came and took the table next to ours As the girl was being seated, she also was reaching for her water glass. She knocked it over and water soaked the table clothe and fell to the tile floor. The cafeteria staff brought a mop to clean up the floor.

Her father took her arm and struck her small hand until it was blood red. This was most upsetting to us. People all over the cafeteria were becoming very upset with his abusive behavior. The father stopped just in time before a table of six large men nearby came over and boxed his ears...

I looked at my wife and children and I just said **Shakespeare.** I was referring to William Shakespeare's, play, **Much Ado About Nothing**?

Some people make a big to do about nothing; we have all knocked over our drink at one time or another in our lives. I am sure that the father was no exception, and had no doubt knocked over his drink a number of times.

When you see something happen in public that is no big deal, but, someone reacts in a disruptive manner, always think or say **Shakespeare, meaning Much Ado About Nothing**.

* * *

BONSAI AND SEQUOIA TREES

These two trees begin their existence from very small seeds. Both seeds weigh less than 1/3000 of an ounce. On the one hand is the bonsai tree of Japan. Soon after the bonsai tree stuck its leaves from the earth, they pull it up. They cut off the tap root and a few feeder roots and then planted it in a small shallow pot, this deliberately stunted its growth.

The seed of the sequoia tree fell on rich earth. Nourished by California rain and minerals it received lots of warm sunshine.

This seed grew to become the great General Sherman that we know today.

It reaches upward to the clouds; it is 272 feet high and 79 feet in circumference.

If we were to cut it down, it would produce enough lumber to build about thirty-eight medium houses,

In the beginning the bonsai and the sequoia were the same size. What made the difference is that the bonsai was stunted

The sequoia tree was not stunted, so it got to it full growth.

It took lots of storms, yes, storms, each storm tested the ability of the root system to hold firm. Sure the tree will sway, may bend very far over. But after the storm has passed the root system has held true.

We will have storms in our life, which test our beliefs Do we hold true to our faith, or do we topple over because our family roots are in a shallow pot, so they can not hold. The big question is did the family roots hold or were they influenced by the wrong ideas. The storm was the true test; we must wait until the storm has passed to know for sure.

Our children can be stunted in their development, in the formative years, or they can grow straight and tall mentally.

It depends on us. Are we always saying "no" to every good thought they have. Many times we say no, go watch television. If we use the television as a baby sitter the children will receive two things from television.

Red eyes and a hollow head.

A better idea is to stop at a store, pick up a few boxes and sit them out in the sunshine. Invite a few of their friends over to play. Then sit back and watch their imagination at work.

Those boxes can build a fort. They can become a train; each child will set in a box, and then you watch to see who becomes the train engineer, as you may be seeing a future leader in the making.

Often they make the boxes into a house. Here as we watch the children show us how they see us as parents they will treat their play children as they see you treat themselves. This can be very enlightening.

The things they will make with a few boxes are endless. Let the children grow and help them to think good thoughts

*   *   *

I DON'T KNOW ASK A GIRL

The other day we saw a young lady wearing a "tee shirt that made a "statement". We asked her what her shirt said. It says "A wise man once said, I don't know, ask a girl".

We have to stop, then think how many times women influenced our young male lives. We males were all greatly influenced by females in the formative years, such as mothers, grandmothers, aunts, sisters, female teachers.

Mother's day is the busiest day of the year for florists, restaurants, and of course, the phone Company. More phone call are placed on Mother than any other day of the year. The moral of this story is, be grateful for your training that came from females, and if you don't know just ask a girl.

God bless my mother, all I am or hope to be I owe to her.

Abraham Lincoln

*   *   *

PERSIST, PERSIST, FOREVER PERSIST

No matter what our goal in life, we use and always remember the four D's because this pushes us ahead to complete our goal. By never giving up we do not tell the world what we can do, we show them. So, persist, persist, forever persist.

That which the mind can conceive and believe it can achieve. Use persistent to the point that you never quit. Achieve it now. Let nothing or anyone cause you to lose sight of your goal. Press on, press on.

*   *   *

BE A LEADER BY EXAMPLE

Take a string, tie a knot in one end and call this end the head. Now place this string on a table, grip the end with the knot and lead it around the table top. See how easy it follows.

Now, stretch the string out and push from the other end. Watch it bow up, just as people will when they are pushed and not being lead.

The whole world is looking for leadership by example. A true leader by example does not just tell the world what they can do, but shows them.

You don't have to go looking for a leader by example, you can become one. It is not hard . All we must do is stay clam while all others are losing their heads around you.

Many years ago a supervisor who was six foot six inches tall and who thought his size was all he needed to influence others to his way of thinking, He fussed at the four young men in his charge plus all others in hearing distance .

He felt that everyone should jump through the hoop each time he snapped his fingers.

The four young men asked this question. "Do you know how long you can be our boss"? His reply was "as long as I like".

Their response was, No, only as long as we will let you and with that all four walked out. They were tired of his verbal abuse. There was no way he could handle all of the business coming there each day by himself. After a few minutes he realized he had made a big mistake. That night he was on the phone begging them to return to work the next day. So, you can be a leader by example even if you are not the boss. Go the extra mile, do more than you are paid for, give 110 %. Always be on time, stay over a few minutes, if needed. Then you are a leader by example. The pay will catch up with you in due time, it always does.

Let us strive to be a leader by example.

If you lead by example many will follow.

MOTIVATION

The world, especially the business world is searching for leaders, not necessarily the old style leaders but a new style known as a leader by example. Not as the leaders of yesterday where they motivated people by fear and intimidation, but a new and different motivation of truly leading by example, the three types of motivation are: number one is **"fear."** for example, "if you are late to work you will be fired."

The second method of motivation is the **"carrot in front of the mule."** this too works great for a short while providing the mule is hungry and the carrot is long enough.

The third method of motivation is by far the greatest of all being **"self motivated."** which is a strong desire to get things done regardless of any and all obstacles they may find in their path. It is almost impossible to slow down or deter a self motivated individual because they are not affected by outside forces; they have determined what can and shall be done and they will find a way.

The new method of leading is by example. The new style boss when the need arises, comes early and stays late. The boss takes time off during a work day for personal business, the same privilege is extended to all employees.

Therefore the survey finds that the work force accomplishes a great deal with more harmony than ever thought possible with the rigid eight to five work schedule, where the employees lived and worked in fear of being fired if they did not adhere to the strict fear motivation.

SAVE YOUR MONEY

If you wish

to set under a

giant oak when

You are older, then

start today by planting a

small acorn on your wedding day.

* * *

MONEY CANNOT BUY EVERYTHING

Therefore, the story goes; in a large city, high in a tall building there was a meeting in progress. The CEO was telling the group at the conference table that money could buy everything. He said if any one would write on paper any thing that money could not buy, and then pass it to him. He would pay $1,000.00 for any item that money could not buy. A young man, who two days before had joined this company, took his pen and paper wrote four items that he felt money could not buy. He passed his note up from the far end of the table; it had to pass through the hands of Vice Presidents Accountants, and the President, to reach the CEO. The CEO studied the paper for about half a minute then took out his pen and check book. He asked the young man his name then wrote him a check for $4,000.00.

We sometimes think money can buy happiness, it cannot. True happiness is not having what we want, but wanting what we have. In the thirties during the great depression, there was little money earned. However, most people were happy. You ask why was this. Because people made dolls using corncobs and material from feed sacks. Some folks did not have a job, so they made Christmas gifts from any thing at hand. They enjoyed life to it fullest. Many children never knew they were poor; love took the place of money.

These are the four things they say he may have wrote on that paper that day (1) the love of a good woman. (2) A baby' smile (3) Good health for you (4) neither can you buy your way into Heaven

* * *

SUCCESS, WHAT CAN I DO
TO EARN IT?

If you could ask each and every young person in America the question "what is success and how does one obtain it?" Their answers would differ by the exact number of young persons asked.

Success is your own goal made into reality in your own life. Live your life to the fullest each and every day, then you are on the road to success. Success is a long journey in which we never arrive until we pass on to our reward. Then people can say "they were a success in life because they did their best to help their fellowman to be successful. One doesn't receive success, you earn it daily. Remember many successes are only temporary. and then we move on to bigger and better goals.

Difficulties happening while on our journey to success will make us think **IF ONLY** these difficulties had not happened at this time These come with out warning and without concern for what happens to us in our life. We ask for many, because we fail to observe the road signs of life. Do this and you will suffer the consequence by receiving difficulties. They often times cause our heart to break, wreck your plans and you think you have nothing to live for.

It is at this time we are quick to say, **IF ONLY** we had taken another road in my journey of life or **WHAT IF** we had not been on this road at this time. This is the opportunity for us to see a new road marker that says **NEVERTHELESS** life goes on.

Just a few days ago I watched as a car pulled up. I turned to a friend and said "I know that young man". He was the person I knew all right, but his life had changed. He now is in a wheelchair and must change his career. He cannot live his life saying **IF ONLY or WHAT IF;** he was bumped by a difficulty of life.

He said "I was on a motorcycle and had a accident, This was after my folks had asked me please do not ride again". so at eighteen I now must ride a wheelchair. I must now live by **NEVERTHELESS** life goes on for me.

Remember to abide by the law and rules in your quest for success. Many top persons in large corporations are going to prison because they did not obey the law or read all of the road signs.

One form of success is just working very hard to help others to get the success they want, then in doing so we will have success.

* * *

WITH EVERY ADVERSITY COMES AN EQUAL OR GREATER BENEFIT WE MUST LOOK FOR IT

A lady in her forties came to see me. After we concluded our business I said, "You look very sad". Her reply was "yes "I received a pink slip today because my Company is downsizing".

My question to her was what is incomplete in your life, what is that one accomplishment you never completed but always wished you could?

She said "I lack one year of completing my college degree, but I never had the time or money". I asked "did your company give you a severance package". Her response was "yes".

Now I knew she had a golden opportunity to return to college and get her degree which she had always desired. Is there anything else to stop you from seeking your hearts desire at this time? With the severance package you now have enough money to last almost two years.

Approximately eighteen months later this lady walked in with a smile from ear to ear.

She asked if we remembered her. Before I could say anything, she told us that she is the lady that we advised to return to college and earn her degree. She said "I did just that, and today I am employed by a large corporation with my salary now twice the amount I was receiving when I was given my pink slip".

She further told us that she took our advice about her adversity and she had found the greater benefit.

We think the world has come to an end when things happen which we do not understand, but wait until tomorrow for it will dawn a new day.

The storm has passed in the night, now we must look for the benefits from the storm. Just think the rain washed all the dust from the leaves, and it removed all the dust from the air. So along with many other benefits we breathe clean fresh air.

With every adversity comes an equal or greater benefit, we must look for it.

IX

THE FOUR D'S PLUS C/R

YOU SAY THIS IS A STRANGE THING TO CONSIDER. . WHAT IS IT? WELL IT IS A FORMULA SO YOU MAY AIM FOR A GOAL IN LIFE AND THIS SYSTEM HELPS YOU TO STAY ON COURSE

1) *Desire:* Knowing what you want in life, then to work daily until it is accomplished. It must be a very strong and never failing desire.

2) *Determination:* Firmness of purpose. This is the act of having a strong resolve.

Resolve "Promise yourself to never quit".

Plus **C**: Commitment: To be totally committed to an idea, so that nothing can stop us..

Having a strong desire to get a goal accomplished, this by setting up a plan. Determination keeps us working on our plan and staying focused on our goal. The word resolve can mean, "Promise yourself to never quit". So, let no one or nothing stop us.

3) *Disappointment:* There will be disappointments in any worthwhile endeavor.

Make all disappointments only temporary never permanent..

4) *Discouraged:* Resolve is needed when people try to discourage you, especially when unforeseeable difficulties happen. This is the time to hold steadfast in your belief.

Your question is what is unforeseeable difficulties. Unforeseeable difficulties are the many pitfalls ahead that you cannot see. They are the many happening that if not handled properly will stop you in your tracks. This is when you remember what *Abraham Lincoln* said and you keep keeping on until you find a way.

Abraham Lincoln said, "Determine what can and shall be done then find a way". The word _shall_ means this is a necessary. The word _should_ means you have a choice; you can or cannot do it because it is up to you. Never use the word should in this quote, *Abraham Lincoln* didn't.

History says no one person has more disappointments in life than *Abraham Lincoln*. There were many times he was discouraged, but he never quit.

You said but he was a great lawyer. True but he was a self-taught lawyer. He was self-taught in everything he tried to do. Yet, he became elevated to the highest office in the land, *President of the United States of America.* Therefore, when you are trying your hardest to reach your goal remember *President Abraham Lincoln* never gave up nor shall you.

Sure, you will make mistakes. We must learn from our mistakes, but, as we have always said. "It is bad to make a mistake; it is far worst when we make the same mistake twice".

Always remember mistakes are really opportunities in work clothes.

You say, how will I know when I am a failure. We will listen to you talk about what happened and if we hear you blame what happened on others and not yourself then we know you feel that you failed in this project .

Failure is instructive. The person who really thinks learns quite as much from his failures as from his successes. *John Dewey*

I always tried to turn every disaster into an opportunity. *John D. Rockefeller*

* * *

THE GREATEST GOLD MINE

So the story goes: a young man struck gold, well, more than just a little gold. He followed this large strike for many months. It made him wealthy.

Then the gold ran out as suddenly as it came. Now our young man had a strong desire to find gold, and he did find gold.

He had determination with some commitment, but not enough to stay on digging and trying to figure out what happened to make the gold disappeared.

So he gave into disappointment. By now he was so disappointed he could not see any way he could go on digging. He became totally discouraged.

He sold out his claim to older miner who thought and said to himself, I know there is still a lot of gold to be found at this strike.

The first young miner did not have the determination, and resolve, which is to promise himself to never quit. Thomas Edison was a person who never quit. If he felt it can be done, he did it.

While in Fort Meyers, Florida, we watched a movie of reporters questioning Mr. Edison as he stood on his porch. One reporter asked Mr. Edison.

"Sir, if you had not found the secret of the electric light bulb, what would you be doing as of right now?" Mr. Edison answered, "young man if I had not found the answer by now, I would still be in my lab searching".

Mr. Edison was disappointed over a thousand times, but determination, and resolve kept him going. He had promised himself to never quit. ***Period.***

The older miner begin to pick in a larger circle for he knew the earth can shift, which would crack the vein of gold and move it up or down and so he continued to dig for about two days and sure enough there it was!.

The older miner had been disappointed many times, but he never lost his resolve thereby not becoming discouraged to the point of quitting.

The older miner worked the mine for many years. History says this was one of the greatest veins of gold ever found. The older miner found it just five feet from where the young miner had quit.

X
LOOK FOR THE
COMPLETE RAINBOW

We travel throughout our life looking for rainbows hoping to find the pot of gold at its end. But all we see is half of the rainbow. The other half is hidden from our view.

This is not because the whole rainbow is not there, but because we just cannot see it from where we are standing.

We had seen many complete rainbows in our life. This is always after a storm. We do not have to even be in the rain storm, but we must be above the area of the storm. We are standing on a mountain top looking down, and then suddenly there is the beautiful complete rainbow. Oh, but the colors are dazzling.

When flying in a plane above a storm, then look down for the complete rainbow. This is how life can be, after adversity has touched our life's then we realize life must go on, at this time look for the complete rainbow, it is there and it can be beautiful. Enough said

ISBN 142510889-X